WOULD YOU RATHER...?

by Justin Heimberg
& David Gomberg

Over **300 crazy questions!**

Terrifically Twisted

Published by Seven Footer Press
247 West 30th St., 11th Fl.
New York, NY 10001
First Printing, January 2012
10 9 8 7 6 5 4 3
Manufactured in Baltimore, Maryland, August 2012

Would You Rather...?® is a registered trademark used under license from Spin Master Ltd.

Cover Design by Junko Miyakoshi
Design by Thomas Schirtz

ISBN 978-1-934734-25-4

www.sevenfooterpress.com

HOW TO USE THIS BOOK

1. Sit around with a bunch of friends.

2. Read a question from the book out loud and talk about it.

You won't believe some of the stuff you'll come up with as you think about which choice to make.

3. Everybody must choose! That's the whole point. It forces you to really think about the options.

4. Once everyone has chosen, move on to the next question.

Would you rather...

have your tongue and the roof of your mouth coated in Velcro

OR

have your armpits coated in double-sided duct tape?

Would you rather...

as an astronaut, throw up in the Space Shuttle

OR

in your helmet during a space walk?

YOU MUST CHOOSE!

WOULD YOU RATHER...HAVE AN IPAD SURGICALLY ADDED TO YOUR THIGH

OR YOUR NOSE ALTERED TO DISPENSE CHOCOLATE VANILLA SOFT SERVE ICE CREAM?

Would you rather...

have to Tweet honestly about your life every 10 minutes

OR

have your parents Tweet about theirs?

Would you rather...

always have an expressionless face

OR

an expressionless tone of voice?
See how long you can go with each!

YOU MUST CHOOSE!

Would you rather...

eat a plate of deep-fried slugs

OR

a salad of moth wings with potato bug bits?

YOU MUST CHOOSE!

Would you rather...

have your toothbrush replaced with a cactus

OR

your toothpaste replaced with super glue?

YOU MUST CHOOSE!

Would you rather...

wink after everything you say

OR

cheek-kiss every single person you meet?

Would you rather...

never be able to use a TV **OR** eating utensils?

a computer **OR** shoes?

doors **OR** chairs?

YOU MUST CHOOSE!

Would you rather...

live in a world where members of Congress and World Wrestling Entertainment exchanged jobs

OR

not?

YOU MUST CHOOSE!

Would you rather...

for $1000, do 10 push-ups **OR** one pull-up?

eat a giant millipede **OR** 40 fireflies?

spell "rhythm" **OR** prove that you have it?

YOU MUST CHOOSE!

Would you rather...

be rooted to the ground like a tree

OR
have to be moving at all times?

Would you rather...

have your voice sound as if there's a bad cell phone connection

OR

have everyone else sound like that?

YOU MUST CHOOSE!

Would you rather...

be a Transformer who changes into a retainer

OR

into a plunger?

YOU MUST CHOOSE!

Would you rather...

during conversation, randomly address people as "Your Honor"

OR

"Soul Brother?"

YOU MUST CHOOSE!

Would you rather...

have a left foot that works as a metal detector

OR

a left hand that functions as a universal remote control?

YOU MUST CHOOSE!

Would you rather...

never be able to say "yes" **OR** "no?"

"stupid" **OR** "smart?"

"resplendent" **OR** "bloated?"

YOU MUST CHOOSE!

Would you rather...

all disagreements with your teacher were settled in the form of battle rap

OR

dance-off?

YOU MUST CHOOSE!

Terribly Twisted

WOULD YOU RATHER...ONLY BE ABLE TO DRINK FROM A FIRE HOSE

OR ONLY BE ABLE TO EAT FOOD THAT'S CATAPULTED INTO YOUR MOUTH

Would you rather...

have a snowball fight against your favorite major league pitcher

OR

not?

YOU MUST CHOOSE!

Would you rather...

live in a maximum security prison

OR

in a giant ant farm?

Would you rather...

compete on *Dancing with the Stars*

OR

force a friend of your choice to compete?

YOU MUST CHOOSE!

Would you rather...

have to carry around all your stuff like a hobo

OR

on a cranky donkey?

YOU MUST CHOOSE!

Would you rather...

have to do your mom or dad's job

OR

have to wear the same outfit as your mom or dad every day?

YOU MUST CHOOSE!

Would you rather...

have an upside-down nose

OR

a vertical mouth?

YOU MUST CHOOSE!

Would you rather...

have your secret crush be revealed in the morning announcements at school

OR

mop the entire school floor over a weekend?

Would you rather...

have one boxing glove hand

OR

two snowshoe feet?

YOU MUST CHOOSE!

WOULD YOU RATHER...HAVE THE ABILITY TO FOLD YOURSELF INTO A PAPER AIRPLANE SHAPE AND GLIDE ACROSS A ROOM

OR INFLATE YOUR BUTT INTO A HOP BALL?

Would you rather...

communicate exclusively by blinking in Morse code

OR

by hand puppet?

YOU MUST CHOOSE!

Would you rather...

be unable to shake the nickname "Generalisimo"

OR

"The Eliminator!"?

Would you rather...

only have your father's childhood video games to play

OR

your father's childhood music to listen to?

YOU MUST CHOOSE!

Would you rather...

burp brown bubbles

OR

fart the sound of glass shattering?

YOU MUST CHOOSE!

27

Would you rather...

have your own lane on the highway

OR

your own checkout line at all stores?

Terminally Twisted

YOU MUST CHOOSE!

Would you rather...

have the ability to zoom in with your eyes

OR

zoom in with your hearing?

YOU MUST CHOOSE!

Would you rather...

have your legs surgically replaced with a pogo stick

OR

your left hand replaced with a head of cabbage?

Would you rather...

have Lady Gaga sing at your wedding

OR

Barack Obama officiate it?

YOU MUST CHOOSE!

Would you rather...

share bunk beds with Mike Tyson **OR** Alex Trebek?

Selena Gomez **OR** Vanessa Hudgens?

a sleep-talking Abe Lincoln **OR** a Lego-obsessed Albert Einstein?

YOU MUST CHOOSE!

Would you rather...

only be able to get anywhere by elephant

OR

by disco dance moves?

YOU MUST CHOOSE!

Would you rather...

be able to shoot dodge balls from your hands at all times

OR

be able to unscrew things with your mind?

Would you rather...

if given a million dollars, spend it

OR

save it?

YOU MUST CHOOSE!

Would you rather...

have your family car's GPS bully you
while giving directions

OR

have the GPS be insecure and need
constant attention and support?

YOU MUST CHOOSE!

Would you rather...

have a 72-hour biological clock

OR

an 8-hour biological clock?

Would you rather...

play this game with Will Ferrell

OR

the Dalai Lama?

YOU MUST CHOOSE!

Would you rather...

have your hands forever stuck as fists

OR

as a double thumbs-up?

YOU MUST CHOOSE!

Would you rather...

constantly move as though treading water

OR

walk around as if limbo-ing?

YOU MUST CHOOSE!

WOULD YOU RATHER...CUT YOUR OWN HAIR WITH A WEED WHACKER

OR CLIP YOUR FINGERNAILS WITH A BELT SANDER?

Would you rather...

have an app that turns your phone into a mirror **OR** a megaphone?

a backscratcher **OR** a Fudgecicle?

a crystal ball **OR** a camera that shows auras?

YOU MUST CHOOSE!

Would you rather...

always be chuckling when not talking

OR

always be humming "You're a Grand Ole Flag"?

Would you rather...

spend an hour in a closed room with a colony of fire ants

OR

with the Kardashians?

YOU MUST CHOOSE!

Would you rather...

move as if playing Dance Dance Revolution while sleeping

OR

freestyle rap while sleeping?

YOU MUST CHOOSE!

WOULD YOU RATHER...EAT A PIZZA TOPPED WITH ALFALFA SPROUTS, BEETS, AND NAIL CLIPPINGS

OR WITH PEPPERONI, SAUSAGE, AND BEETLES?

Would you rather...

have a Slurpee-dispensing belly button

OR

produce peanut butter fudge ear wax?

YOU MUST CHOOSE!

Would you rather...

have a super-human sense of smell but a nose 10 times larger than the one you have now

OR

super-human hearing with ears 10 times larger than your ears?

Terminally Twisted

YOU MUST CHOOSE!

Would you rather...

have your birthday party in a highway rest area bathroom

OR

a dentist's office during your check-up?

Would you rather...

gain 30 pounds

OR

gain five pounds all in your face?

YOU MUST CHOOSE!

WOULD YOUR RATHER... HAVE TO USE A GARDEN RAKE FOR A FORK

OR A CHAIN SAW INSTEAD OF A KNIFE?

Would you rather...

roll up into a ball like an armadillo when scared

OR

shake your butt in the air like a rattlesnake when threatened?

YOU MUST CHOOSE!

Would you rather...

lose your lunch on a roller coaster

OR

lose your swimsuit at a waterpark?

Would you rather...

have an itch you can never scratch

OR

a tickle you can never stop?

Terminally Twisted

YOU MUST CHOOSE!

Would you rather...

post all your report cards on Facebook

OR

all your love letters?

Would you rather...

be able to camouflage yourself like a chameleon

OR

puff up your body like an inflatable parade float?

YOU MUST CHOOSE!

Would you rather...

see things blurry

OR
be blurry?

Would you rather...

be principal of your school

OR
not?

YOU MUST CHOOSE!

Would you rather...

be three feet tall yet able to dunk a basketball

OR

seven feet tall yet unable to jump?

YOU MUST CHOOSE!

WOULD YOU RATHER...HAVE ALL YOUR SCHOOL CLASSES TAUGHT BY WORLD LEADERS

OR PROFESSIONAL WRESTLERS?

Would you rather...

be video chat buddies with Tom Brady

OR

with a Muppet of your choice?

YOU MUST CHOOSE!

Would you rather...

get a tattoo on your tongue **OR** your forehead?

your palm **OR** the back of your hand?

a wedding ring tattooed on your finger when you get married **OR** a picture of a crushed bug tattooed on the bottom of your foot?

YOU MUST CHOOSE!

Would you rather...

have your dreams written by Rick Riordan

OR

Jeff Kinney?

YOU MUST CHOOSE!

Would you rather...

have nacho cheese saliva

OR
steel wool body hair?

Would you rather...

have an Xbox game based on your life

OR

your life based on an Xbox game of your choice?

YOU MUST CHOOSE!

Would you rather...

sweat 1000 times the normal amount

OR

sneeze four gallons of snot?

Terrifically Twisted

YOU MUST CHOOSE!

Would you rather...

spend a night in a *Toy Story*-esque Toys "R" Us

OR

in Narnia?

YOU MUST CHOOSE!

Would you rather...

give a high five

OR

an old-school low five?

YOU MUST CHOOSE!

Would you rather...

wear swim goggles for 24 hours straight

OR

wear your pants backwards for 24 hours?

YOU MUST CHOOSE!

Would you rather...

be able to flatten yourself like a cartoon character

OR

be able to extend your eye around corners?

YOU MUST CHOOSE!

Would you rather...

have Wolverine-like claws made of cheap plastic-ware knives

OR

Superman-like heat vision that can only be used to make Jiffy-Pop?

YOU MUST CHOOSE!

Would you rather...

have a huge bumblebee stinger on your butt

OR

have a frog's tongue in your mouth?

YOU MUST CHOOSE!

Would you rather...

have a camel hump on your back that allows you to go days without water

OR

have porcupine quills you can fire off at people?

YOU MUST CHOOSE!

WOULD YOU RATHER...GET FACIAL HAIR ON THE UPPER HALF OF YOUR FACE

OR HAVE A TURKEY WATTLE HANGING FROM YOUR NECK?

Would you rather...

audibly burp between every word you speak

OR

fart with every step you take?

Would you rather...

leave visible finger paint splotches on everything you touch

OR

leave visible footprints wherever you go?

YOU MUST CHOOSE!

Terrifically Twisted

Would you rather...

have lightsaber fingernails

OR

Jedi mind trick ability?

Terrifically Twisted

YOU MUST CHOOSE!

Would you rather...

produce snot that changed colors depending on your mood

OR

poop that changed colors?

Would you rather...

eat food regurgitated from your mom like a baby bird

OR

only be able to sleep outdoors in a giant bird nest?

YOU MUST CHOOSE!

Would you rather...

wear a suit of armor for a month straight

OR

full scuba gear?

YOU MUST CHOOSE!

Would you rather...

have to store all your clothes in the freezer

OR

have to wear all your food for a day before eating it?

YOU MUST CHOOSE!

Would you rather...

have your most embarrassing picture posted on 100 billboards

OR

have the most embarrassing thing you ever said be a popular ringtone?

YOU MUST CHOOSE!

Would you rather...

have the powers of Harry Potter **OR** Percy Jackson?

Superman **OR** Green Lantern?

Aquaman **OR** a superhero version of George Washington Carver named Peanut Man? (Use your imagination.)

YOU MUST CHOOSE!

Would you rather...

have a debilitating fear of school bells **OR** sea shells?

snow cones **OR** ear phones?

the word "walk" **OR** the word "talk"?

YOU MUST CHOOSE!

Would you rather...

have glow-in-the-dark eyeballs

OR

eyes that can be removed and used for ping pong balls?

Would you rather...

have an alarm clock that wakes you with a slap across the face

OR

by slowly wetting your bed?

YOU MUST CHOOSE!

Would you rather...

have helium-filled boogers

OR

helium-filled poops?

YOU MUST CHOOSE!

Would you rather...

shower in honey

OR

bathe in sloppy joe?

YOU MUST CHOOSE!

Would you rather...

always be the age 7

OR

27?

YOU MUST CHOOSE!

Would you rather...

instantly grow a mustache if you can't answer a question

OR

begin to fart loudly when you lie?

YOU MUST CHOOSE!

Would you rather...

live in a world where it snows hard-boiled eggs

OR

where it rains glue?

Would you rather...

change your name to any number

OR

any weather forecast?

YOU MUST CHOOSE!

WOULD YOU RATHER...HAVE A WARDROBE MADE COMPLETELY OUT OF WICKER

OR FRUIT ROLL-UPS?

Would you rather...

have twice your IQ but twice as big of a head

OR

half your IQ with a normal-size head?

YOU MUST CHOOSE!

Would you rather...

talk like a robot for the rest of the day

OR

move like a robot?
Try it!

YOU MUST CHOOSE!

Would you rather...

spend three months confined to an amusement park

OR

confined to your house?

YOU MUST CHOOSE!

Would you rather...

greet everyone with a headlock and noogie

OR

say goodbye to everyone with a long, drawn-out hug?

YOU MUST CHOOSE!

Would you rather...

win a Grammy **OR** an Oscar?

an Emmy **OR** a sports MVP award?

the award for "Best Shadow" **OR** "Most Likely to Come in Second?"

YOU MUST CHOOSE!

Would you rather...

have half of anything you drink leak out of a dimple on your chin

OR

eventually come out as armpit sweat?

YOU MUST CHOOSE!

Would you rather...

have an echo that translates what you say into Russian

OR

that corrects your bad grammar?

YOU MUST CHOOSE!

Would you rather...

live in a world where everyone looks the same

OR

not?

YOU MUST CHOOSE!

Would you rather...

have your school named after you

OR

be able to name the school anything else?
What would you name it?

YOU MUST CHOOSE!

Would you rather...

eat Oreo cookies with anchovy stuffing

OR

Milky Way bars with toothpaste filling?

YOU MUST CHOOSE!

Would you rather be reincarnated as...

a horse that hates the outdoors **OR** a hawk that's afraid of heights?

a bowling pin **OR** a golf ball?

a lemur **OR** a certified public accountant?

YOU MUST CHOOSE!

Would you rather...

have inverted feet (they face backward)

OR

have an inverted face (things that stick out get sucked in and vice versa)?

YOU MUST CHOOSE!

Would you rather...

only be able to communicate at all times
in 140 characters or less

OR

in rhyme?

YOU MUST CHOOSE!

Would you rather...

go to a school where people break into song
like in *Glee*

OR

where superhero-like battles happen every day?

Would you rather...

have a Muppet based on you

OR

a Smurf based on you?
What would the Smurf be named?

YOU MUST CHOOSE!

Would you rather...

be able to control the world like you can control an Xbox Kinnect game

OR

be able to write the script for your life every Friday?

YOU MUST CHOOSE!

Terrifically Twisted

Would you rather...

share a locker with the Riddler

OR
Magneto?

Would you rather...

sneeze marbles

OR
fireflies?

YOU MUST CHOOSE!

Would you rather...

always have the five-block radius around you covered in a thick fog

OR

always be 100 degrees?

YOU MUST CHOOSE!

Would you rather...

never be able use the letter "j"

OR
the letter "q"?

YOU MUST CHOOSE!

Terminally Twisted

Would you rather...

eat the contents of a pepper shaker **OR** a salt shaker?

a bottle of ketchup **OR** a bottle of mustard?

a jar of mayonnaise **OR** a bag of flour?

DO NOT TRY THIS AT HOME!

YOU MUST CHOOSE!

Would you rather...

talk in Auto-Tune

OR

only speak through speech balloons?

YOU MUST CHOOSE!

Would you rather...

have Yoda as your hairstylist

OR

Optimus Prime as your chauffer?

YOU MUST CHOOSE!

Would you rather...

be trapped in a stalled elevator with your worst enemy

OR

with five dogs that have bladder control problems?

YOU MUST CHOOSE!

Would you rather...

your gym teacher be Simon Cowell **OR** the WWE's Kane?

Drew Brees **OR** Jack Black?

Taylor Lautner **OR** The Blue Man Group?

YOU MUST CHOOSE!

Would you rather...

grow up to be like Lady Gaga **OR** Michelle Obama?

Aaron Rodgers **OR** Zac Efron?

Mark Wahlberg **OR** Mark Zuckerberg?

your math teacher **OR** your reading teacher?

YOU MUST CHOOSE!

Would you rather...

be followed around by a 1940's newspaper journalist who excitedly writes down everything you do and keeps saying "What a scoop!"

OR

have every room you enter have the same painting of a stern old woman whose eyes always follow yours?

YOU MUST CHOOSE!

Would you rather...

be able to mute other students

OR
teachers?

Would you rather...

suffer from the unpickable wedgie

OR

the unscratchable itch?

YOU MUST CHOOSE!

WOULD YOU RATHER...HAVE TO CUT ALL THE GRASS ON A FOOTBALL FIELD WITH SCISSORS

OR ZAMBONI AN ENTIRE ICE RINK WITH AN ICE SCRAPER AND SQUIRT GUN?

Would you rather...

wear an outfit made out of taffy

OR
birdseed?

Would you rather...

have eyes that look like egg yolks

OR
teeth that look like candy corn?

YOU MUST CHOOSE!

Would you rather...

have a different accent every day

OR

a different height?

YOU MUST CHOOSE!

Would you rather always have to wear...

300 necklaces **OR** 300 Band-Aids?

suspenders **OR** combat boots?

jeggings **OR** a clown nose?

YOU MUST CHOOSE!

Would you rather...

fart while giving a presentation in class

OR

during a first kiss?

YOU MUST CHOOSE!

Would you rather...

get gum stuck in your hair

OR

hair stuck in your gum?

YOU MUST CHOOSE!

Would you rather...

have parents who taught life lessons in haiku

OR

in song-and-dance routines?

YOU MUST CHOOSE!

Would you rather...

be able to staple things with your mouth

OR

be able to turn any piece of paper into a Post-It note?

YOU MUST CHOOSE!

Would you rather...

have a scar in the shape of a question mark

OR

a bull's-eye?

YOU MUST CHOOSE!

Would you rather...

brush your teeth with bug guts

OR

the world's hottest hot sauce?

YOU MUST CHOOSE!

Would you rather...

wear a wasp nest mitten

OR

spiderweb underwear?

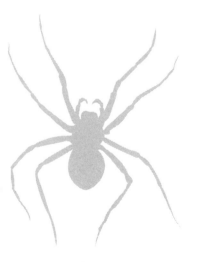

YOU MUST CHOOSE!

Would you rather...

eat a grilled-toe-cheese sandwich

OR

a BLT (beetle, larvae, and tentacle sandwich)?

YOU MUST CHOOSE!

Would you rather...

suck the air out of things around you when you yawn

OR

shatter things around you when you cough?

Would you rather...

get a zit the size of a peppercorn on your nose

OR

a zit the size of a tennis ball on your hip?

YOU MUST CHOOSE!

Would you rather...

see a sport that was a combination of competitive eating and pole-vaulting

OR

boxing and Nascar?

YOU MUST CHOOSE!

Who would you rather have on your basketball team...

Spiderman **OR** Batman?

Harry Potter **OR** Percy Jackson?

LeBron James **OR** Gandalf?

YOU MUST CHOOSE!

If you were an NFL player, after scoring a football touchdown, would you rather celebrate by...

doing a Tim Tebow **OR** a raucous dance?

digging in the end zone like a dog **OR** "owling" on the goal post crossbar?

putting the ball under your shirt like you're pregnant **OR** passionately kissing the referee?

YOU MUST CHOOSE!

Would you rather...

be adopted by Brad Pitt and Angelina Jolie

OR

Tom Brady and Gisele?

Would you rather...

drink cola carbonated by a horse's farts

OR

milk "chocolatized" by the ink squirted from a live squid?

YOU MUST CHOOSE!

Would you rather...

get to school by unicycle

OR

in a giant hamster ball?

YOU MUST CHOOSE!

Would you rather...

read a real book  an eBook?

read on a Kindle **OR** an iPhone?

listen to an audio book **OR** take a "book pill" where after you swallow, you understand what was in the book over a period of 4-6 hours, but then forget it?

YOU MUST CHOOSE!

Would you rather...

have your car seat double as a toilet

OR

not?

Would you rather...

only be able to eat yellow foods

OR

foods that start with "a"?

YOU MUST CHOOSE!

Would you rather...

get a paper cut on your tongue

OR

in between your toes?

YOU MUST CHOOSE!

Would you rather...

have a skunk that does your bidding

OR

a tiger?

YOU MUST CHOOSE!

Would you rather...

every full moon turn into a were-ostrich

OR

no matter where you are, every Thursday at 1pm, become convinced you are on the game show *Jeopardy*?

YOU MUST CHOOSE!

Would you rather...

eat a watermelon where all the seeds were spider egg sacs

OR

a jar full of olives stuffed with boogers?

YOU MUST CHOOSE!

Would you rather...

get a headache every time you see a puppy

OR

faint every time a fly lands on you?

Would you rather...

have a premium speaker system installed in your butt

OR

a fog machine?

YOU MUST CHOOSE!

Would you rather...

have a compulsive need to bury your leftovers in the backyard like a dog burying a bone

OR

have the need to chase a laser pointer like a cat?

YOU MUST CHOOSE!

Would you rather...

suddenly turn any stairs you set foot on into an escalator going down

OR

be able to turn any bathroom into an elevator?

Would you rather...

have farts that sound like an important news bulletin

OR

Christina Aguilera yodeling?

YOU MUST CHOOSE!

Would you rather...

only be able to blink 50 times in a day

OR

only be able to take 50 steps?
(You will be grounded for a month if you exceed the number.)

YOU MUST CHOOSE!

Would you rather...

play a game of soccer in a field where the grass is 4 feet high

OR

play a game of basketball on a giant Slip-N-Slide?

YOU MUST CHOOSE!

Would you rather...

be stuck in a life raft filled with a boa constrictor

OR

the cast of *Jersey Shore*?

Would you rather...

have perfect table manners but call everyone by the name "Sweetiepants"

OR

have the ability to tie shoes super fast but cry a little every time you do it?

YOU MUST CHOOSE!

Would you rather only be able to travel by...

tiptoeing **OR** country line dancing?

leapfrogging **OR** conga line?

tricycle **OR** slingshot?

YOU MUST CHOOSE!

Would you rather...

always have the north side of your body covered in moss

OR

have hair that blooms daffodils in the spring?

YOU MUST CHOOSE!

Would you rather...

when you blow your nose, have a blowtorch flame shoot from your nostril

OR
Jazz music?

Would you rather...

have every chair you sit in make a loud farting noise when you sit down

OR

always silently pass gas for real when you sit down?

YOU MUST CHOOSE!

Would you rather...

never be able to eat a meal unless it is served on a Backyardigans placemat

OR

unless it is served with caviar?

YOU MUST CHOOSE!

Would you rather...

have tiny groundhogs living in your pores

OR

tiny bats living in your nostrils?

YOU MUST CHOOSE!

Would you rather...be able to magically style, grow, and control your hair by thought

Or be able to control Justin Bieber's hair?

WOULD YOU RATHER... COMPULSIVELY PET APPLIANCES AS THOUGH THEY WERE PUPPIES

OR TEASE LAMPS MERCILESSLY LIKE A PLAYGROUND BULLY?

Who would you rather have as your school principal...

Willy Wonka **OR** Dumbledore?
James Bond **OR** Sherlock Holmes?
your mom **OR** your dad?

YOU MUST CHOOSE!

Would you rather...

have to privately rehearse every sentence you say before you can speak it correctly to someone

OR

always take a dramatic bow after everything you say?

YOU MUST CHOOSE!

Would you rather...

have trading cards printed depicting all the most embarrassing moments of your life

OR

have a mime follow you for one day a week mocking everything you do?

YOU MUST CHOOSE!

Would you rather...

squeeze a big pimple on your face and have it burst with banana pudding

OR

a laser light show?

Would you rather...

have 30 extra pounds of fat that you can shift around your body but never lose

OR

10 huge pimples on your face that you can shift around but never remove?

YOU MUST CHOOSE!

Would you rather...

have anything you draw come to life

OR

anything you write about actually happen?

YOU MUST CHOOSE!

Would you rather...

fight 10 hole punchers **OR** 1000 toothpicks?

100 helium filled balloons **OR** 100 swarming pairs of socks?

four moody warlocks **OR** nine chivalrous hockey goalies?

YOU MUST CHOOSE!

Would you rather...

have your face on all four sides of your head

OR

have your face on three sides of your head, and on the fourth side, the face of former Philadelphia Eagle Harold Carmichael?

YOU MUST CHOOSE!

Would you rather...

be allowed to wedgie the school principal in front of the whole school

OR

be allowed to slap the school bully with no consequences?

YOU MUST CHOOSE!

Would you rather...

salute everybody you meet

OR

have to stand up and make a sentimental toast every time you drink a beverage?

YOU MUST CHOOSE!

Would you rather be horribly allergic to...

Spanish **OR** sarcasm?

people with one-syllable names **OR** shoes?

things that cost less than $19.95 **OR** things that are colder than 80 degrees?

YOU MUST CHOOSE!

Would you rather...

be able to type 400 words per minute

OR

be able to speak 400 words per minute?

YOU MUST CHOOSE!

155

Would you rather...

have stegosaurus spikes jutting out of your spine

OR

a rhino horn sticking out of your forehead?

YOU MUST CHOOSE!

Would you rather share a bedroom with...

a moody lynx **OR** a bee colony?

25 vampire bats **OR** five wolverines?

four warthogs **OR** Snooki?

YOU MUST CHOOSE!

Would you rather...

have skin with the texture of pineapple

OR

skin covered in suction cups?

YOU MUST CHOOSE!

Would you rather...

go to the dentist once a month

OR

never go to the dentist (but pay for it in dental problems)?

YOU MUST CHOOSE!

Would you rather...

only be able to leave your house on Wednesdays

OR

only be able to leave your house dressed as Chewbacca?

YOU MUST CHOOSE!

Would you rather...

have the intense desire to "knight" people whenever you hold a knife during your meals

OR

feel the unquenchable need to start "the wave" whenever you take public transportation?

YOU MUST CHOOSE!

Would you rather...

have skin coated in poison like a poison dart frog

OR

produce 1,000 gallons of sweat each day?

Would you rather...

sleep for a year in an overcrowded chicken coop

OR

eat food from a crowded pig trough?

YOU MUST CHOOSE!

Would you rather...

be able to color using your fingertips

OR

have the power to float 1 foot off of the ground?

YOU MUST CHOOSE!

Would you rather...

always wear your underwear on the outside of your clothing

OR

be unable to tell the difference between dodge balls and muffins?

YOU MUST CHOOSE!

Would you rather be restricted to eating things that are...

hot **OR** cold?

square **OR** circular?

liquefied **OR** moving?

YOU MUST CHOOSE!

Would you rather...

have a fly's eyeballs

OR

an anteater's nose?

YOU MUST CHOOSE!

Would you rather...

never get another homework assignment

OR

have unlimited free App downloads?

YOU MUST CHOOSE!

Would you rather...

be able to read your teacher's mind

OR

have the power to turn invisible for 1 hour per day?

Would you rather...

use roadkill for your pillow

OR

cobwebs for a blanket?

YOU MUST CHOOSE!

Would you rather...

only be able to enter vehicles through the windows

OR

have to sleep across your bed?

YOU MUST CHOOSE!

169

Would you rather...

wake up every day with a new family

OR

with a new face?

YOU MUST CHOOSE!

Would you rather...

eat without using your hands

OR

type without using your hands?

YOU MUST CHOOSE!

Would you rather...

be unable to miss a basketball free throw

OR
always throw a strike?

YOU MUST CHOOSE!

Would you rather...

play Simon Says with Duane "The Rock" Johnson

OR

compete in a spelling bee against The Undertaker?

YOU MUST CHOOSE!

Terribly
Twisted

Would you rather...

have oatmeal for sweat

OR

hair gel for saliva?

Would you rather...

be able to hole-punch paper by sitting on it

OR

have a functioning Ouija board on your stomach?

YOU MUST CHOOSE!

Would you rather...

foam up with bath suds whenever you are lying (getting more bubbly the more you lie)

OR

lose all the effects of gravity whenever you're called on in class and don't know the answer?

YOU MUST CHOOSE!

Would you rather...

forget how to chew

OR
forget how to sit?

Terrifically Twisted

YOU MUST CHOOSE!

Would you rather...

eat a black-ant-berry pie

OR

a dry-ice-cream cake?

YOU MUST CHOOSE!

Would you rather...

produce a tsunami any time you sneeze

OR

a tornado any time you burp?

Would you rather...

know everything your parents ever thought

OR

have them know everything you thought?

YOU MUST CHOOSE!

Would you rather...

be able to toast bread by holding it tightly in your armpit

OR

have the power to boil eggs by holding them in your mouth for 3 minutes?

YOU MUST CHOOSE!

Would you rather...

wake up each morning with a different shoe size

OR

with a different mustache?

Would you rather...

have no joints in your body

OR

3,400 joints distributed randomly?

YOU MUST CHOOSE!

Would you rather...

have your emotions work in reverse

OR

your digestive track?

Terrifically Twisted

YOU MUST CHOOSE!

Would you rather...

have only your right nostril

OR

only your bottom lip?

Would you rather...

only be able to bathe in your kitchen sink

OR

go to the bathroom in it?

YOU MUST CHOOSE!

Would you rather...

have the power to read and understand any language

OR

know the precise outcome of any sporting event before it happens?

Would you rather...

eat a caramel-and-booger-crusted apple

OR

pancakes drenched in St. Bernard slobber?

YOU MUST CHOOSE!

183

Would you rather...

have Charlie Sheen as your school psychologist

OR

Gordon Ramsay as your cafeteria worker?

Would you rather...

only be able to sing in the shower

OR

in Pig Latin?

YOU MUST CHOOSE!

Would you rather...

have skin made of a flexible version of dry erase board material

OR

made of corkboard?

YOU MUST CHOOSE!

Would you rather...

live in a world where the ocean was made of chocolate milkshake

OR

where snow was actually marshmallow?

Would you rather...

have to travel south in the winter

OR

move further west each year?

YOU MUST CHOOSE!

Would you rather...

literally go whichever way the wind is blowing

OR

literally always march to the beat of a different drummer?

YOU MUST CHOOSE!

Would you rather...

always look like you just brushed your teeth and forgot to rinse

OR

like you never washed the shampoo out of your hair?

Would you rather...

psych yourself up before taking a test with a gorilla-like, chest-pounding show of strength

OR

by slamming into your classmates like football players before a game?

YOU MUST CHOOSE!

Would you rather...

cheat

OR

fail?

Would you rather...

live in a world where kids spin a cocoon when they turn 10 and then emerge in a few weeks as 30-year-olds

OR

where babies are born as fish-like creatures who evolve over a few years to humans?

Would you rather...

have a 1 hour school day

OR
a 3 month school year?

YOU MUST CHOOSE!

Would you rather...

in one sitting, eat 10 Big Macs

OR

100 buffalo wings?

Would you rather...

have bushes shaped like you in your front yard

OR

a pool shaped like whatever you want in your backyard?
What shape would you choose?

Would you rather...

have anything you type into Wikipedia become true

OR

have all knowledge in Wikipedia?

Would you rather...

have an alarm that wakes you up by pie-to-the-face

OR

that insults you, getting meaner the longer you stay in bed?

YOU MUST CHOOSE!

Would you rather...

be attached to your home with a 1-mile-long bungee cord

OR

be attached to your best friend with a 10-foot-long bungee cord?

Terribly Twisted

Would you rather...

be able to "bookmark" your favorite places and teleport there with the click of a mouse

OR

be able to download three-dimensional objects?

YOU MUST CHOOSE!

Would you rather...

be able to teleport your bowel movements from your intestines to a toilet

OR

to anywhere but a toilet?

Would you rather...

have an eye on the bottom of your foot

OR

where your belly button is?

YOU MUST CHOOSE!

Would you rather...

have your nostrils function as a double-barrel shotgun

OR

as a vacuum?

YOU MUST CHOOSE!

Would you rather...

have caterpillar-cocoon earrings

OR

a live-tarantula pendant?

Terminally Twisted

YOU MUST CHOOSE!

Would you rather...

have the force but only when making breakfast

OR

be able to read minds but only when people are thinking about lettuce?

Would you rather...

have the ghost of Einstein as a tutor

OR

Derrick Rose as your private basketball coach?

YOU MUST CHOOSE!

Would you rather...

when thinking, have the Mac computer "spinning beach ball" appear by your head

OR

"thinking music" play?

Would you rather...

have your back be a popular target for graffiti artists

OR

your head be a popular target for birds?

YOU MUST CHOOSE!

Would you rather never get...

a headache **OR** a stomach ache?

picked on **OR** spit on?

scared **OR** angry?

YOU MUST CHOOSE!

Would you rather...

have webcams placed in your least favorite teacher's house

OR

tons of mousetraps placed in her/his house?

YOU MUST CHOOSE!

Would you rather...

have the Avengers as your bodyguards

OR
the X-Men?

Would you rather...

have lifelong free airfare

OR

lifelong free doughnuts?

YOU MUST CHOOSE!

Would you rather...

fight crime with a pet starfish

OR

a pet hamster?

Would you rather...

sleep in 5 minute bursts

OR

5 day marathon sessions (total sleep time in a month is the same)?

YOU MUST CHOOSE!

Would you rather...

have to dress like your math teacher

OR

talk like your English teacher?

YOU MUST CHOOSE!

Would you rather...

sleep a night in a dumpster  a chicken coop?

on a balcony without a railing on the 100th floor **OR** on the shoulder of a highway?

on bologna sheets **OR** on a bed of bleu cheese?

YOU MUST CHOOSE!

Would you rather...

frown when you're happy and smile when you're sad

OR

laugh when you're angry and clap when you're scared?

YOU MUST CHOOSE!

Would you rather...

be raised by penguins **OR** beavers?

owls **OR** prairie dogs?

giraffes **OR** Kardashians?

YOU MUST CHOOSE!

Would you rather...

catch a finger in a mousetrap

OR
a toe?

YOU MUST CHOOSE!

WOULD YOU RATHER...PRODUCE EGGS WHEN YOU COUGH

OR EMIT A SMALL MUSHROOM CLOUD EVERY TIME YOU FART?

Would you rather...

be able to sleep with your eyes open

OR

talk without moving your mouth?

YOU MUST CHOOSE!

Would you rather...

be able to answer any question when called on in school but only in impressions

OR

be able to answer any question correctly on a written test, but only when adding a sentence insulting your teacher?

YOU MUST CHOOSE!

Would you rather...

have a gym unit in "planking"

OR

pro wrestling?

Would you rather...

use slug-tipped swabs

OR

a tiger claw backscratcher?

YOU MUST CHOOSE!

Would you rather...

use a spiked blowfish as a pillow

OR

a hornet's nest?

Would you rather...

bite into a Snickers where the nuts were beetles

OR

bite into a Butterfinger where the inside was grass clippings?

YOU MUST CHOOSE!

Would you rather...

have a luxury recliner chair at your school desk

OR

your own private bathroom?

Would you rather...

get all your knowledge simply by downloading "updates"

OR

be able to access other people's thoughts by connecting to them with a cable?

YOU MUST CHOOSE!

Would you rather...

take a class in cartoon analysis

OR
sandwich criticism?

Would you rather...

get Justin Bieber's autograph

OR

get to shave his head?

YOU MUST CHOOSE!

Would you rather...

always talk like you are at the dentist and they are working on your teeth

OR

always walk like you are walking down the aisle of a fast moving train?

Would you rather...

have a toilet made from a shark's mouth

OR

a bathtub made from a whale's bladder?

YOU MUST CHOOSE!

For Even More Difficult Choices and Deranged Dilemmas, Get the *Would You Rather...?*™ Board Game

"Would you rather wake up every day in a new city, or with a new face?" In the Would You Rather...? Board Game, there are no right-or-wrong answers, just difficult decisions! Figure out how others will answer, and you're on your way to winning. Based on Justin & Dave's best-selling books, Would You Rather...? is the perfect party game! From Spin Master™, for ages 12 and up, 3 or more players.

Not fully grossed out yet?

Still wishing for more weirdness?

Look for these other *Would You Rather...?* books featuring hundreds of deranged dilemmas.

www.sevenfooterpress.com

YOU WON'T BELIEVE YOUR EYES!

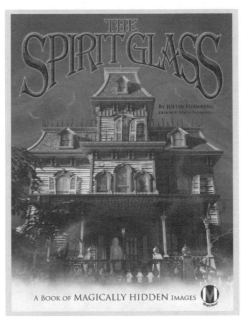

As you slide the Spirit Glass across the page, strange things begin to happen... Ghosts emerge from the mist, images take shape in crystal balls, secret messages magically appear. For each of twelve imaginative spreads, you must use the Spirit Glass to confront the challenge before you: Find ten ghosts in a haunted house. Search for nine skeletons hidden by the graveyard sky. Uncover hidden messages in invisible spider webs. If you do, you just might unlock the power of... The Spirit Glass!

 TheSpiritGlass.com

Go online to TheSpiritGlass.com and use the book to solve a supernatural mystery full of riddles, challenges, and puzzles. Winners will be eligible to be used as a ghost in a future book.

Ⓜ Seven Footer Kids

SEE THE UNSEEN!

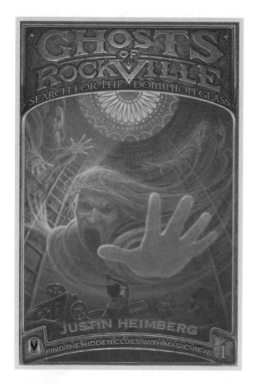

Become a ghost hunter with MagicView™, an amazing, new, interactive reading experience unlike anything you've ever seen (or haven't seen!) before. Now you can live out the adventure, joining the characters as they reveal fingerprints, peer into crystal balls, or stare down the ever-changing face of a menacing apparition. Each hidden image is another clue in an awesome supernatural mystery that will amaze readers of any age.

GhostsofRockville.com